0702159

W9-ATI-581

0 1021 0213320 3

ON LINE

FIRST AMERICANS
The Huron

DAVID C. KING

 **Marshall Cavendish**
Benchmark
New York

ACKNOWLEDGMENTS

Series consultant: Raymond Bial

Marshall Cavendish Benchmark
99 White Plains Road
Tarrytown, New York 10591-9001
www.marshallcavendish.us

Text copyright © 2007 by Marshall Cavendish Corporation
Map and illustrations copyright © 2007 by Marshall Cavendish Corporation
Map and illustrations by Christopher Santoro

Library of Congress Cataloging-in-Publication Data
King, David C.
The Huron / by David C. King.
p. cm. — (First Americans)
Includes bibliographical references and index.
ISBN-13: 978-0-7614-2251-8
ISBN-10: 0-7614-2251-X
1. Wyandot Indians—History—Juvenile literature. 2. Wyandot
Indians—Social life and customs—Juvenile literature. I. Title.
II. Series: First Americans (Benchmark Books (Firm)
E99.H9K56 2006
971.4004'97555—dc22
2006011970

Photo research by Joan Meisel
Cover Photo: Dennis MacDonald/Alamy
The photographs in this book are used by permission and through the courtesy of:
Alamy: 21, Philip Scalia; Corbis: 34, William Manning; 38, Bettmann; 42, Wally McNamee;
North Wind Picture Archives: 4, 6, 7, 8, 9, 13, 14, 22, 30, 40; Raymond Bial: 16,18, 24, 25, 28; Robert Holmes: 1.

Editor: Tara Koellhoffer
Editorial Director: Michelle Bisson
Art Director: Anahid Hamparian
Series Designer: Symon Chow

Printed in China
1 3 5 6 4 2

CONTENTS

1 · THE PEOPLE OF THE NORTHERN FORESTS

In the year 1534, a French explorer named Jacques Cartier sailed up the St. Lawrence River. He and his crew were the first Europeans to travel so far into the interior of North America. They passed forests that stretched for hundreds of miles from the Atlantic coast west to the Great Lakes and beyond.

At first, this wooded landscape looked like a vast wilderness. But then Cartier's ship came to clearings where there were large towns of people known as Huron Indians. Each town was protected by **stockades**—walls made of upright logs. Inside the stockades, bark-covered longhouses were arranged in neat rows. Some Huron towns had nearly 200 houses, with more than 4,000 people.

Outside the stockades, the Huron women and girls tended fields of corn, beans, squash, and pumpkins. The men

Jacques Cartier made four voyages to North America. He hoped to find a water route through the continent to reach Asia.

added to the food supply by hunting and fishing with bows and arrows and spears. They hunted big game such as deer, bears, and moose, as well as smaller animals, including squirrels, rabbits, and opossums. Men and boys often hunted in groups of forty or more. When they found a group, they drove the animals toward a central corral, where they killed as many as they needed.

A number of villages formed a **clan**, usually with people

Even small Huron villages were protected by stockades.

who were related to one another in some way. The combined clans and villages formed the powerful Huron League, which controlled large parts of what are now the Canadian provinces of Quebec and Ontario.

From Trade to Troubles

When the Huron saw Cartier's ship, they welcomed the strange men with their pale skin and "thunder sticks" (guns). Other Frenchmen came, and they began a thriving trade with the Huron. The French had discovered that furs from the

The Huron were friendly to the Europeans but were also curious about their pale skin.

New World's beavers made perfect **felt** for men's hats. The Huron were delighted to provide thousands of beaver pelts in exchange for guns, iron cooking kettles, knives, and tools made of steel.

The Huron enjoyed this trade for about 100 years. They sometimes formed alliances with the Europeans against their

A group of Huron brings furs to trade with Europeans.

rivals. In 1609, for example, another French explorer, Samuel de Champlain, had Huron warriors with him when he discovered the lake that is now named after him. When they met a band of Iroquois Indians, Champlain ordered his men to shoot them. The incident led the Iroquois to resent the Huron and want revenge.

The Huron were no match for the powerful Iroquois warriors who attacked in 1648–1650.

The 1600s became a nightmare for the Huron. The Europeans brought diseases, such as smallpox and measles, which often killed the Indians. When a European disease reached a Huron town, it quickly turned into an epidemic that could wipe out the entire community. In the early 1500s, the Huron population was estimated to be between 30,000 and 45,000 people. By 1650, disease had reduced the population to around 10,000 people.

A second form of disaster struck in the years 1648–1650. The Huron's bitter enemies, the Iroquois, launched a surprise

The Huron lived in the region around the Great Lakes.

attack. More than 1,000 warriors stormed through the Huron towns, setting the long-houses ablaze, killing people and forcing the survivors to flee into the forests.

About 300 Huron escaped to an area near the modern city of Quebec. Hundreds more fled westward and wandered for years in the lands around the Great Lakes. These people, along with refugees from smaller tribes, became known as the Wyandot. Many eventually settled in Kansas, while another group moved to Indian Territory (now the state of Oklahoma). Many of the Huron who survived the fighting and diseases were absorbed into the tribes of the Iroquois Confederation, also known as the Iroquois Confederacy or the Iroquois League. The Huron bands that survived in Quebec, Kansas, and Oklahoma have tried to keep alive some of the traditions of their culture.

Hiawatha

According to legend, a Huron (some say he was an Onondaga) named Deganawidah left his people and joined the Iroquois. With a follower named Hiawatha, who was a member of the Mohawk tribe, he convinced the leaders of the Iroquois tribes to form the Iroquois League as a way to stop the almost constant warfare among the tribes. The plan worked, and the league of the five Iroquois tribes became the strongest and most durable of all Indian alliances.

The bitter conflict between the Huron and the Iroquois is part of the story in James Fenimore Cooper's famous novel *The Last of the Mohicans*.

According to legend, Hiawatha was able to slay sea monsters with his bow and arrows. He helped form the Iroquois League.

2 · THE HURON WAY OF LIFE

The Huron lived by farming, and also hunted, fished, and gathered wild foods. The men cleared the fields for crops, burning brush and vines and loosening the soil with digging sticks. The women planted, tended, and harvested the crops, which included corn, squash, beans, pumpkins, and sunflowers. The only crop the men grew was tobacco, which was used for special ceremonies. While the women took care of the gardens, the men went on hunting or fishing trips and sometimes formed war parties to fight another tribe. They also went on journeys for trade.

Preparing Foods

Making cornmeal was an important daily chore for Huron women. They stripped the corn kernels off the cobs, using a

A Huron woman plants corn in small mounds, while her husband watches.

scraper made from a deer's jawbone, then they poured the corn into a hollow-log kettle. Next, the women added scoops of lye, a powder made from boiled ashes.

Using two sticks, Huron women lifted stones from the fire and dropped them in the kettle. Soon the water was steaming and bubbling. When the skins were softened, they scooped the corn into a special basket that was so tightly woven, it

A hollow-log kettle and hot stones were used to cook much of the Huron's food.

held water without leaking. After rinsing the corn in the water basket, they spread the kernels to dry.

When the corn was dry, they placed it in a hollowed-out log and went to work pounding and grinding the kernels with a rounded stone. Finally, the bowl was half full with finely ground yellow meal. The women could now use the meal to make mush or form it into flat cakes that were topped with maple syrup, honey, or animal fat.

In the late summer and through the autumn, Huron women worked to store food for the coming winter months. Some corn was left on the cob, placed in large baskets, and stored in large pits underground. Other ears were sun dried, then hung from the beams of the longhouse.

Squash was cut into strips or rings, dried in the sun, and also hung in the longhouse. The sun was used to dry sunflower seeds, beans, berries, grapes, and wild roots and blossoms. These items were stored in baskets along with nuts and herbs.

Indian Foods

The Native Americans who lived in the woodlands of the Northeast enjoyed a healthy diet and a great variety of foods. Corn was their most important food. The northeastern tribes grew more than fifteen kinds of corn, which were used in many different dishes.

The Woodland Indians called corn, beans, and squash the "three sisters," because they were grown together. The bean vines climbed around the cornstalks, and the large squash leaves shaded the soil and kept it moist. Beans were also highly nutritious, since they were rich in protein and vitamins. Fish and meats provided essential elements of the diet.

Corn was a very important part of the Huron diet. It was dried to preserve it for several months.

Daily Life

During the days, Huron women and children were in the fields and many of the men were hunting. Groups of around eight families lived together in a longhouse. The building was quite dark. Smoke from the cook fires rose high into the rafters and out through smoke holes in the roof. The only light came from the two doorways and the smoke holes. Along the walls were rows of wooden benches. The lower benches were covered with furs and used for sleeping. The wide upper benches were used for storage.

The Huron people normally ate whenever they were hungry rather than at set times, but the largest meal was usually eaten in the late morning. The men ate first, then the women and children.

Stew and different forms of cornmeal were available most of the time. After a successful hunt, the people stuffed themselves with roasted meat. Some of the meat was cut into strips and smoked over a low fire. Part of the preserved meat was pounded into powder, then mixed with fruit and animal fat to make a food called **pemmican**. Pemmican could be kept for months without spoiling and was especially useful when traveling because it was easy to carry and was packed with nutrients.

Maple Magic

The Huron collected the thick sap that flowed from maple trees. In the spring, the Huron cut slits through the bark and inserted a cedarwood spout that allowed the sap to flow into birchbark containers. The sap was boiled for hours until it became a rich syrup that could be used for several weeks. With more cooking and stirring, the syrup turned into sugar. This maple sugar was stored in cone-shaped birchbark containers for use throughout the year.

Maple syrup and maple sugar were the Huron's favorite forms of sweetening. Either could be added to stews and breads, or spread on meat or fish. Honey and syrup made from cooked berries were also used often.

Woodland Craftsmen

Huron men were skilled craftsmen. They made many items, including the bows and arrows they used while hunting. After examining branches of beech, oak, and hickory trees, a Huron man would select a good one to make a strong bow. The man then cut and trimmed the branch. Over the next few days, he heated the wood over a low fire, bent it, polished it, then heated it and polished it again. Finally, he had a beautiful bow. He cut notches at either end and

The Huron used birchbark containers to collect maple sap. Today, metal or plastic pails are used.

The moon provided plenty of light for Huron hunters.

wound deer sinew into a single long bowstring.

Huron men made arrows from straight pieces of wood that they collected and dried. Feathers from crows, vultures, turkeys, and hawks were tied to one end of the arrow to keep it from wobbling in flight. A carefully made flint arrowhead was tied to the other end.

Huron men also made birchbark canoes. Although the Huron usually traveled on foot, for long distances they used canoes on rivers or lakes.

They made the canoe of white birch, and for a frame,

Recipe: Maple Cornbread

This recipe is based on two of the most important Huron foods: corn and maple syrup, along with a few modern ingredients for easier preparation.

Ingredients

- 1 cup yellow cornmeal
- 1 cup flour
- 3 teaspoons baking powder
- 1/2 teaspoon salt

- 1 egg
- 3 tablespoons melted butter
- 1/2 cup pure maple syrup (not artificial)
- 3/4 cup milk

Equipment

- 2 mixing bowls
- wooden mixing spoon
- fork or wire wisk
- small saucepan

- 9 x 9-inch nonstick baking dish
- table knife
- adult helper

Makes 4–5 servings

1. Remember to have an adult with you when you use the stove or oven. Preheat the oven to 400 degrees.
2. In one mixing bowl, combine the cornmeal, flour, baking powder, and salt.
3. Break the egg into the other bowl and stir it with a fork or wire wisk.
4. Have the adult help you melt the 3 tablespoons of butter in a small saucepan. Or put the butter in a microwavable dish and microwave it for about 20 seconds.
5. Add the butter, maple syrup, and milk to the bowl with the beaten egg. Stir to mix the ingredients.
6. Pour the liquid mixture into the bowl of dry ingredients. Stir well but do not beat.
7. Pour the batter into the baking dish. Bake at 400 degrees for about 20 minutes. When the top is a light golden brown, your maple cornbread is done. Allow the cornbread to cool for a few minutes, then cut with a table knife and serve.

they used white cedar. They used wedges and a hammer to split the cedar into thin boards. All the men worked together to make a frame of cedar boards and poles, which they placed between the sheets of birchbark. They pulled up the bark and laced it to the frame with long, thin root fibers. The bow and stern came to a sharp point and were slightly raised to protect against waves on stormy lakes. The thin cedar boards formed

Every detail had to be perfect to make a birchbark canoe.

the inside bottom of the canoe, and all the seams were sealed with resin from black spruce trees. A well-made canoe would provide swift transportation for many years.

Clothing and Jewelry

Traditional Huron clothing was simple and comfortable. Deerskin was the most common material, trimmed in cold weather with bits of rabbit or squirrel fur. Men wore a **breechcloth** over a belt, usually with leggings attached. A shirt or cape and moccasins completed the

Hours of work were needed to prepare a deerskin to be made into clothing.

Bear-Claw-Bead Necklace

Almost all Native American tribes made necklaces out of animal claws and bones as well as bits of seashell, clay, and stone. Contact with Europeans introduced brightly colored beads that were quickly put to use in Indian crafts.

The necklace you'll make using self-hardening clay is copied from a style used by both the Huron and Iroquois. Both boys and girls can wear these necklaces, or you can use yours as a wall decoration.

You will need:

- several sheets of newspaper
- waxed paper and masking tape (optional)
- 1 package of self-hardening clay
- ruler
- knitting needle or large nail
- acrylic paints, bright colors for the beads and brown for the bear claws
- small paintbrush
- 20-inch rawhide lace (sold as shoelaces), or twine
- adult helper

1· Spread several sheets of newspaper on your work surface. You may find it helpful to tape a large sheet of waxed paper on the newspaper; this will keep the newspaper ink from smearing the clay and your fingers.

2· Open the package of clay and knead it with your hands for a few minutes to make it softer and easier to work with.

3· Break off a small piece of clay and form it into the shape of a bear claw—about 1¹/₂ inches long and less than 1/4 inch thick. Younger kids

Bear Claw — 1 1/2 inches

Bead — 1/2 inch

should have an adult help them use a knitting needle or a large nail to make a hole for stringing in the upper part of the claw.

4· Make 4 or 5 more claws the same way.

5· Break off a small piece of clay and form it into a round ball, about 1/2 inch thick. Again, you may need an adult to help you make a hole through the bead.

6· Make 11 more beads the same way.

7· Allow all the pieces to dry, following the instructions on the package of clay.

8· Use a small paintbrush and acrylic paints to paint each item: The bear claws should be brown, and the beads should be 4 or 5 different colors. The pieces will be easier to paint if you hold each on the knitting needle or nail.

9· Allow the paint to dry.

10· Thread each piece onto the rawhide lace or twine, placing two beads between the claws.

11· Tie the ends of the rawhide into a tight double knot. Your bear-claw-and-bead necklace is now ready to wear or display.

Huron Necklace

Feathers, porcupine quills, and other items were used to decorate furs.

outfit. Women wore a skirt with a cape or a sleeveless dress. Leggings that reached to the knees were also common. In the summer, both men and women wore much less clothing.

Clothing was beautifully decorated. Almost every piece of deerskin clothing had fringed edges. Huron women were highly skilled in sewing dyed porcupine quills and shell beads onto garments and moccasins. Floral and geometric designs were often painted on clothing.

Contact with Europeans, beginning in the mid–1500s, brought changes in the clothing of all Native American peoples. Glass beads became valuable trade items. Before long, clothing, moccasins, deerskin bags, and other items were decorated with beautiful and intricate designs created with these beads. European cloth was also a welcome innovation. Cotton and other fabrics were easier to sew than deerskin. Most Huron began to wear a combination of traditional and European-style clothes and decorative items.

The Huron were also fond of face and body paint, and wore some kinds of jewelry. During feasts and ceremonies, both men and women put bright paint colors on their faces and bodies. Their favorite forms of jewelry were necklaces and headbands made of snakeskin.

3 · HURON CUSTOMS AND BELIEFS

Huron culture is based on what is called an "oral tradition." This means that there was no written language and no books of laws or police to enforce laws. Instead, the people lived according to their customs and traditions, and each generation learned from the elders. All Huron people knew their place in the community and what was expected of them.

Children and Family Life

Most families had only two or three children, and they were brought up with affection and firmness. All members of the family, including grandparents, aunts and uncles, and cousins, helped raise the children.

From an early age, children began to learn the skills they

Special chants and dances were used by shamans to cure sickness.

would need as adults. Girls learned to tend crops, gather and store wild foods, prepare meals and preserve foods for the winter, and cure animal hides to make soft, comfortable clothing. Boys learned by watching older men hunt, fish, and make tools and weapons. They became skilled at making and using tools from wood, flint, animal bones and sinews, and seashells. Every item the Huron made was fashioned with an eye for beauty as well as function. A food storage bag might be decorated with porcupine quills; a paddle for stirring food would have an elegantly carved handle.

Even the games children played had a learning purpose in addition to fun. Boys learned about both cooperation and competition with team games, and developed other skills through games such as throwing a spear at a rolling stone. Girls learned to cut and sew deerskin clothing for wooden dolls before making life-sized garments. On long winter evenings, families sat around the fire and listened to grandparents or great-grandparents tell stories about the tribe's history, legends, and myths.

Tribal Government

Before the arrival of the Europeans, the Huron people had formed a loose confederation that stretched along the St. Lawrence River to the eastern Great Lakes. It consisted of more than a hundred towns. Each town held people related by blood, following the mother's line, not the father's. One or more towns formed clans, and the clan mothers chose male representatives, or **sachems**, to serve in the confederacy's council. The council members met regularly to resolve disputes among the clans and towns.

This system worked well until the arrival of European diseases and the attacks of the Iroquois. From 1650 on, each Huron tribe survived as best it could, with the western tribes, now known as Wyandot or Wyandotte, moving often to survive.

The Huron Story of Creation

The Huron believed that their land was an island at the center of the world. The island rested on the back of a giant turtle.

Tobacco was hung up to dry. It was smoked as part of special ceremonies.

The Importance of Tobacco

Like most Native American societies, the Huron believed that everything had a soul, including rocks, trees, the crops, and the sun, moon, and stars, as well as wild plants and animals. One way to maintain harmony with this spirit world was by making offerings of tobacco.

Another shared belief was that tobacco had special powers. Smoking it in a long pipe called a **calumet** was believed to increase a person's wisdom. Consequently, at ceremonies and tribal councils, the men sat in a circle and passed the calumet in a clockwise direction. Although the pipe was used in all sorts of meetings, including war planning, Americans and Europeans called it a "peace pipe" because it was smoked when fighting ended.

The world began when Aataentsic, the mother of humankind, fell through a hole in the sky. The great turtle, which swam in an endless sea, saw what had happened and ordered sea creatures to swim to the bottom of the ocean and dredge up soil to pile on his back. The fish and other creatures obeyed and built up Earth so that Aataentsic landed softly on the new place.

When Aataentsic landed, she gave birth to two sons: Iouskeha and Tawiscaron. Iouskeha created the rivers and lakes, made good weather, made the corn grow, and let the animals out of a huge cave so humans could hunt them. Tawiscaron, however, caused disease and death. Iouskeha and Aataentsic lived together in a bark house far to the west. They sometimes appeared at Huron festivals disguised as humans. Iouskeha could also appear in dreams to tell whether the harvest would be good or poor.

Healing

The Huron believed illness had to do with both the body and the mind. A major role of religion was to try to heal both kinds of illness. The art of healing was in the hands of the village **shaman**.

To understand the sick person's illness, the shaman usually began by asking about the individual's dreams or visions, looking for some clue about either the cause or the cure for the disease. Over many generations, shamans had built up a wealth of knowledge about the healing properties of various herbs.

Some healing ceremonies were quite elaborate, with beating drums to put the shaman in a trance, dances, and feats of magic. Every winter, the Huron had a soul-curing ritual called the Ononharoia. The festival involved feasting, wild dances by masked performers, and the exchanging of gifts. The hope was that those who were ill would regain their health.

4 · THE LONG HURON JOURNEY

From 1650 on, the Huron story was a struggle to survive. With their numbers reduced by disease and the power of the Iroquois, the Huron became a scattered people.

One group managed to live peacefully in the southwest corner of Ontario province in Canada. The Canadian government gave the Canadian Wyandot a **reserve** near Amherstburg. After struggling for many years, this branch of the tribe began to enjoy some prosperity. Today, there are about three thousand Canadian Wyandot.

Other bands of Huron fled to the west and wandered through the Great Lakes region during the late 1600s and the 1700s. They lived for short periods in present-day Wisconsin, Minnesota, and Michigan. In the early 1700s, a large group settled in Ohio.

Chief Pontiac was one of the leaders who managed to unite several tribes to try to hold back American settlers.

Throughout the 1700s, many Huron joined other tribes who were fighting to hold back the steady advance of Europeans and Americans. Huron warriors took part in the Indian uprisings against the British and Americans led by Chief Pontiac in 1763 and the Shawnee Tecumseh in 1810–1813. They also joined the British in fighting the Americans during the American Revolution (1775–1783).

The Shawnee warrior Tecumseh was killed while fighting on the side of the British in the War of 1812.

Defeats in these conflicts only made the Huron weaker.

In the 1800s, American settlers pushed westward, forcing Native Americans to give up their traditional lands. In 1830, the U.S. Congress passed the Indian Removal Act, which ordered all eastern tribes to move west of the Mississippi River to land called Indian Territory. The Huron had to give up their lands in Michigan, Wisconsin, and Ohio.

Many Huron settled in Kansas Territory, but this land was opened to settlers only ten years later. The Huron worked out two solutions that have lasted to the present: One group moved to present-day Oklahoma, where they are now recognized as the "Wyandotte Tribe of Oklahoma." The other group bought land in Kansas and built a community named Wyandot City. They welcomed non-Indians and, within a decade, several towns were combined and renamed the community of Wyandotte. The community became a model of how nonnatives and Native Americans could live together peacefully. In 1886, the name was changed again, this time to Kansas City, Kansas.

The American Indian Movement (AIM), which included many Huron, led marches to demand greater opportunities for Indians.

Slowly, from the late 1800s to today, the Huron people gained a measure of peace. Over time, the U.S. government changed its policies toward Native American tribes. In the late 1800s, the policy was to force the Indians to live like Americans. That policy was finally reversed in the 1930s. In the 1960s, during the civil rights movement launched by African Americans, some Huron demanded greater equality. Gradually, the American government began to recognize that many Indian people, especially those on the **reservations**, were living in terrible poverty.

Government programs, beginning in the 1970s, provided funds to improve schools, open health-care clinics, and create new job opportunities.

Like other Native Americans, the Huron have found renewed pride in their rich heritage. The descendants of the great Huron tradition in Kansas, Oklahoma, and Canada have all held gatherings, called **powwows**, inviting people of all backgrounds to come and sample Huron dances, foods, stories, and crafts. The goal of Huron tribal leaders is to involve more young people in learning about and practicing their traditions.

· TIME LINE

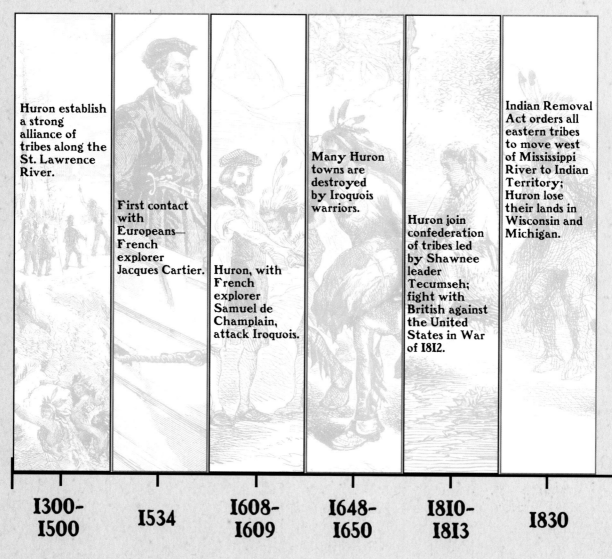

Huron establish a strong alliance of tribes along the St. Lawrence River.

First contact with Europeans— French explorer Jacques Cartier.

Huron, with French explorer Samuel de Champlain, attack Iroquois.

Many Huron towns are destroyed by Iroquois warriors.

Huron join confederation of tribes led by Shawnee leader Tecumseh; fight with British against the United States in War of 1812.

Indian Removal Act orders all eastern tribes to move west of Mississippi River to Indian Territory; Huron lose their lands in Wisconsin and Michigan.

1300–1500   1534   1608–1609   1648–1650   1810–1813   1830

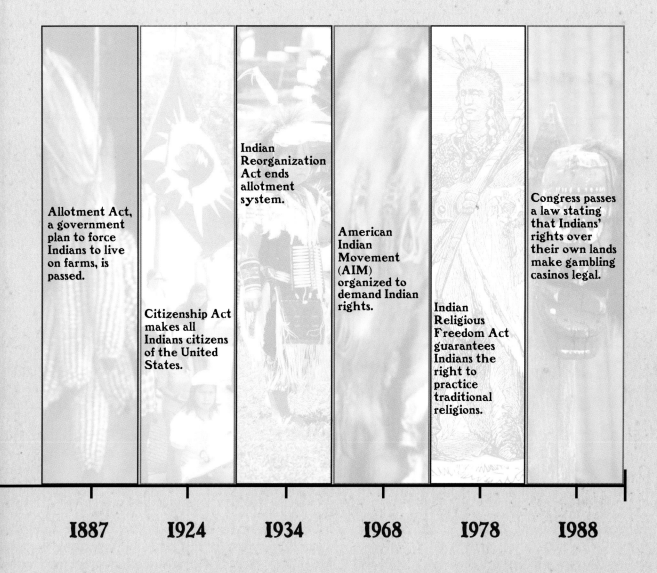

Allotment Act, a government plan to force Indians to live on farms, is passed.

Citizenship Act makes all Indians citizens of the United States.

Indian Reorganization Act ends allotment system.

American Indian Movement (AIM) organized to demand Indian rights.

Indian Religious Freedom Act guarantees Indians the right to practice traditional religions.

Congress passes a law stating that Indians' rights over their own lands make gambling casinos legal.

1887   **1924**   **1934**   **1968**   **1978**   **1988**

· GLOSSARY

breechcloth: Garment worn by men that reaches from the waist to the upper thigh.

calumet: Huron pipe for smoking tobacco; called "peace pipe" by Americans and Europeans.

clan: A group made up of related families.

felt: Fabric made from beaver fur.

pemmican: A nutritious food made of powdered meat mixed with fruit and animal fat.

powwow: A social gathering that includes traditional dances.

reservation: An area of land set aside by the U.S. government as a home for Native American tribes.

reserve: The Canadian term for "reservation."

sachems: Male tribal leaders chosen by the women clan leaders.

shaman: A person with special healing powers.

stockades: Solid walls built around Indian villages, made of upright logs; also known as palisades.

· FIND OUT MORE

Books

Carlson, Laurie. *More Than Moccasins: A Kid's Activity Guide to Traditional North American Indian Life*. Chicago: Chicago Review Press, 1994.

Libal, Autumn. *Huron.* Broomall, PA: Mason Crest Publishers, 2003.

Murdoch, David. *Eyewitness: North American Indian*. New York: DK Publishing Co., Inc., 2005.

Speare, Elizabeth George. *The Sign of the Beaver*. Boston: Houghton Mifflin Company, 1983.

Web Sites

www.geo.msu.edu/geo333/hurons.html

www.nativeculture.com

www.nativeculture.com/huronindians.html

www.nativetech.org

About the Author

David C. King is an award-winning author who has written more than forty books for children and young adults, including *Projects About Ancient Egypt* in the Hands-On History series. He and his wife, Sharon, live in the Berkshires at the junction of New York, Massachusetts, and Connecticut.

· INDEX

Page numbers in **boldface** are illustrations.